FORBIDDEN: THE SELECTED POEMS OF PHOENIX GIBSON

FORBIDDEN: THE SELECTED POEMS OF

PHOENIX GIBSON

Dedicated to those that remain by my side.

Contact information

Instagram – phoenixgibson__

Email – Burningphoenix2004@outlook.com

Introduction

Thank you to everyone that has joined me on my poetry journey. This book is a collection of poems I've written between the ages of 16-19. It does not contain every single poem written during those years but rather a curated selection I thought best for this collection. This was originally supposed to be a standalone book filled with strictly new poems but because of where I'm currently at in life, I've been too depressed to consistently write new poetry. And as a result of this and me being unsure of when I will be back to my old routine, I've decided to instead release a collection of poems to compensate for this uncertainty. This also gives me a chance to revise old poems I've grown dissatisfied with. Thank you again for joining me on this journey.

-Alex

Table of contents

Table of contents

Scars

Another part of a messed-up game

Immortality

Sometimes I feel defeated

Fantasies

Closing

The store

The store

I am the store you come to visit

Accepting your drop-ins without hesitation

And at the moment of your arrival

Switching into full operation

My love for you stands indefinitely

And so,

I ask myself, "Will you marry me?"

Knowing that your preferred method is shoplifting

Bits and pieces of humanity

I grow more infatuated every second

But colder after every visit

Love is a dream

Love is a dream

I'm unsure I want to achieve

For the sake of preserving

Its mythology

For such a thing is

Unimaginable to me

I cannot

Even begin to comprehend

Life

With this new addition

Its concept is foreign

And I am much too used to rejection

Creation

When we all die in the end

I need for there to be

A reason for creation

My head is filled with inconsistencies

My beliefs move from one place

To another

Why is there something

Rather than nothing?

Why have noise

When there could be silence?

So many unanswered questions

A relic from the past

It's funny to think that

Had I caught you at an earlier date

Maybe we could have stood a chance

But every woman I have ever met

Had already attended the funerals

Of who they used to be

And now my love is a relic

From the past

Long since obsolete

I wish I knew how

I could have loved

Any differently

Our reality

Our reality is

Overshadowed

By my dreams

When I close my eyes

Your love does not feel

So out of reach

The fantasy life

When I looked into your eyes

I thought I could see my future once

In my mind, I would often visualize

And picture the wedding night

And moment by moment

I would live an entire hoax life

Centered around the idea

That it was you who was meant to help spend my life

But when you looked at me

Somewhere

Accompanied by all the happiness of this fantasy life

Came the realization that

It was a price you weren't willing to pay

And when you began to look away

The fantasy land began to fade

My deceived heart having given way

Loving for both of us

I came to you

In search of me

Despite us having

Separate identities

I thought that if you could love me

Then I could learn to love me too

I didn't know that I would be stuck

Trying to love for both of us

A dream I'm afraid to wake up from

If I had known sleep was just death being shy

I may never have stopped to rest here

How was I supposed to know

That the moment matter became conscious

It would become fearful of being switched off again?

That it would have become fond of the moments

It has spent among the living?

To love, hug, and experience

The wonders of existence

Only to be met with the realization that

It has to come to terms with knowing

It's part of an experiment

That eventually all things must come to an end

This is a dream I am afraid to wake up from

I tried to look death in the eye

I tried to look death in the eye

I cried crimson tears

And her eyes met mine

"What brings you here?" she asks

"I just wanted to catch up with an old friend", I reply

A jovial interaction

She asks me how I'm doing, how I've been

I tell her, "same old, same old"

She looks at me with a shameful face

Peace washes over me

And a razor blade

That story you hate to tell

If we never talk again

I hope the memories we shared guide you well

I'm fine with being that one story you hate to tell

If it helps you on your journey

Towards becoming

A more complete version of yourself

Love is a razor blade

Love is a razor blade

That does not demonstrate

Mutual feelings

Instead, it glides about the skin

Haphazardly

Unwilling to submit to

Any sudden impulses

Times I'm afraid

There are times I'm afraid

I'm going to lose you

My mind starts racing

And all I can think about

Are all the mistakes I've made

The mess I've put you through

But then I remember

All the times I've made you smile, hugged, and laughed with you

And deep down I know everything will be ok

Because whenever I am feeling worried

You always show up unexpectedly

And make my whole day

An unconscious transfer

We swapped mindsets

But mine was already set

I felt contempt

With what was in my head

But instead

You transferred to me

Your contents

After a part of me realized

You might be onto something

And now I am left juggling additional assets

Including a possible hidden vision

I now thought I couldn't see

Meanwhile,

You are beginning to reach the same conclusion

I had originally

And now when I look at you,

I see me

A love unforgettable

Every day with you has started to feel like midnight

The way the light refuses to illuminate your face

And when you speak

I dance to the remix of an old song

I can't recall how the original goes

But it has started to grow on me

When you hold my hand

It feels more like I'm holding it for you

And ever since you started wearing gloves

I can't remember the exact texture

From when they last touched

I thought that once things had ended

I could move on

But the memories have only faded with age

The feelings still remain

One thing

What am I besides a body

When all it takes is one thing

To become absent of all which give you notoriety?

You can have it all

But still come up short

By one thing that ties it all together

And its as though

You never had anything at all

If it kept you by me, I would change my appearance

Maybe then my love would matter

But until then,

I will continue to daydream of the day

You finally take your walls down

A version of you

It took a while for me to figure out

I fell in love with a version of you

That did not exist

You gave me a quick glimpse

And left my mind to fill in the gaps

I saw what I wanted to

And you gave me full control over the fantasy

You helped me create

A flake of snow

A single flake of snow

Was enough to warn

The oncoming of a storm

Surely, I knew

As evidenced by the crow

And the way it squawked and
withered in the cold

The way the snowflakes,

One by one gathered by the
window

Causing it to freeze up

And chip away

As if chiseled

Or maybe it was the way the
temperature outside

Read below zero

All I know is,

As I peered through the
window,

I was greeted by the same
crow that had warned me

As still as a tree

All had gone silent outside

As all the people that had
once roamed

Now like the crow

Statues

Pilgrims

Love is not ours to command

We are pilgrims

Embarking on a voyage

Towards unknown land

Moving to and from

In search of a suitable destination

Uncertain of where it will leave us

In the end

Are we ever truly lonely?

I embrace loneliness

As if it's the woman of my dreams

We've grown quite fond of one another

She's the only one that gets me

I can tell her anything

And be at peace knowing

She'll always be right here with me

After all

As long as we can be our own companions

Are we ever truly lonely?

1st impressions

I fear I haven't yet shown
you the best sides of me

We talk and talk but I never
know

Which side I should show

I fear I've only shown you
the worst sides

Whereas there's a lot more to
me than that

Sides that only certain people
have met

But I'm afraid you don't care
to get to know the rest

Given that first impressions
are often seen as

Being all that there is

Having to justify my whole
character

In only a few sentences

And I don't know

Given by what's already
known

If I will get the freedom

And the opportunity

To let my full intentions be
known

And be granted the luxury

Of being able to day by day

Build up

And expand on our
relationship

Reality is not a dream

I fell in love with the way

I wanted you to treat me

But you showed me

Reality is not a dream

Ignorance

If I had someone to call mine

Maybe my response would have been

Different

But I walk this earth alone

And so,

I make do with blissful ignorance

I know no sentiment

Of the boundless limits

Of affection

Infinitely more lonely

You occupy my mind

As if it were yours

But I'm just as lonely

Maybe even more than before

But take away my thoughts

And I am contempt with the world

And this is despite being

Infinitely more lonely than before

The world I envision

For me and you

Is beyond what imagination

Is capable of rendering

I may never understand the complete picture

My love for you

Extends beyond what

Our mortal forms are capable of

You are all that is needed

Every moment with you

Makes me question existence

Because if the whole world were like this,

Nothing else would make sense

Why keep on building

When you are all that is needed for fulfillment?

The whole world disappears

When I'm in your presence

Superficial appearances

Love does not exhibit

Human characteristics

So how can you hope to

Control it

When all you can do

Is maintain

Superficial appearances?

Deep down

You know this isn't love

So why are you trying so hard

To convince yourself

That it is?

What do you have to gain from this?

I become the broom

Sometimes,

I become the broom to my own mess

Trying my best to sweep away the cracks

And in-between the crevices

For the hope of

Fixing something too deeply broken

To ever be fixed on its own

Or through companionship

When eventually, down the road,

I realize

That I am not on my own

But this is something I sometimes do by my lonesome

Because in this moment

I feel as if I am the problem

Fate

If it's meant to be

It'll be

So why do I attempt

To defy destiny?

It's a losing battle

But still, I insist in

Not going down without fighting

It's silly

And a bit foolhardy

But at the end of the day

At least I had a say

In what fate had decided for me

Death

Death is being gone

For the time being

A short break

In-between

The next leg

Of your journey

A coming-of-age party

The road back

I often like to look back on the road

And see the mess I've made

The cracked cement helping lead the way

Back towards suppressed memories,

Left to decay

But as I walk the path,

I start to experience vivid hallucinations of the past,

Making my whole body run cold with emotion

The chills engulfing my soul

As I get a clear view of

All I've done wrong

But it hurts to look for too long

So, before you know it,

I'm back up the road

A stroll through time

I wander through time

Not knowing when I'll arrive

I speak to you

And then head off back into

The great divine

You are my concept of time

All there is, is death

All there is, is death

Petty arguments

And grudges

Just don't fit in

I have no need for them

Wherever I'm going

Perpetual motion

I long for you

But not of your presence

I long for the idea

Of what my love for you

Represented

Hope, acceptance, and new beginnings

I long to have found someone

For my feelings to have mattered

But my life remains in perpetual motion

Luxury

Life bore no expense to me

Because luxury is

Being able to breathe

Many seek wealth

Without knowing

Of its true abundancy

We are already in

Affluent supply

Of the riches we need

Its rather unfortunate

We still suffer from greed

Loneliness

Having you here means

Loneliness is able to remain dormant

For a little while longer

I have yet to identify

The exact cause of it

But that doesn't mean

Your love isn't valid

You're the light that shields me

From everything

There is to fear about the darkness

And if I could spend every second with you

It would always be daylight

Why you stay quiet

People that were once open
to closed-minded individuals

Are the reason they now
choose to be quiet

The reason why you don't
open up to people that ask

Even if they are genuinely
concerned

And want to tackle this
emotional task

You've been around the
wrong people

All they wanted to do was
shut you down

And drop you

Just for saying what was on
your mind

They talked bad about you,

Gossiped about you,

But still, you didn't mind

You thought it was normal
and would pass in time

But as time went on,

They wanted you to grow
into the monster they saw
you as

They wanted others to see the
picture they painted you as

And when it didn't show,

They still dropped you for
coming too close

For showing your innermost

And so, to this day

You still find it difficult to
open up to those that are
close

The town center

We brush past each other

On our way towards

The town center

You're teeming with life

And I'm on the way out

You and I can both feel it

We acknowledge each other

In silence

Like a couple of distant friends

I nod a thanks to you

And you nod a thanks to me

You've a long road ahead of you

With much to see

And much to do

I hope the sights treat you as well

As they did me

And then we both head towards the unknown

What becomes of you?

If I am to be

The very thing you made me

Then what becomes of you

And the

Image that constitutes

For everything that is beautiful

About the world?

I cannot rid myself of

The elements

That have already been

Established for beauty

Beauty took a unique approach with you

Beauty took

A unique approach with you

You're unlike anything I've ever

Encountered

A level above dreams

You're that thought at the

Back of the mind

That refuses to be let out

A passive state of consciousness

I can never seem

To catch a glimpse of

An eye opener

To what beauty really is

And I'm finally awake to see it

When I am alone

My heart longs for another soul

Another body to keep me warm when times are cold

Because it is hard to carry on when you are alone

Sometimes, you need another soul to confide in

Another voice to ask you why you cry

To tell you that everything is going to be alright

Because maybe if we had that voice to confide in

A lot of us wouldn't want to die

We wouldn't cry bitter tears

And we wouldn't look towards the sky

Asking why we are alive

We would already have the answers in that which we confide

That special someone

That would be with us until we die

I never gave hatred the time of day

I saw the world

Through sorrowful eyes

But never gave hatred

The time of day

Death was an inevitability

That would have hindered me

Had I chosen to string things along

Love was the unattainable goal

That kept me going

Endless paragraphs

You used to be someone

I could sit down and write endless

Paragraphs for

But it took until I finished the first couple of books

To realize

You didn't even put enough effort in

To finish a sentence

Scars

Scars

Scars may be skin deep

But mine are at a level

Most seem unwilling to reach

The distance is miniscule

But has ever only been enticing to those

Looking to take a short vacation

The collection of collagens that bind the skin

Have always been more numerous

Than those willing to

Venture past its creation

In the end,

The distance equates to the bonds severed

Race

I wish I could experience

Independent happiness

But my mind deems every situation

A feeling of separation

And I am left with only independence

The identifying marker being

The color of my skin

Mankind's long outdated misconception

Turned solution

I guess we forgot about us all being human

December 25th

This is the only day of the year

I can say I got a tree

Just so I could watch it blossom

With you

Ornaments upon ornaments

And stockings too

With gifts like these

What else do I need?

Because memories upon memories

We'll make them too

I cannot imagine this day without you

Merry Christmas

It seems like every year

The list of people I say "Merry Christmas" to

Gets shorter and shorter

A fantasy not meant to be

I like to believe

There will come a day

When I don't fall asleep with you

Fresh on my mind

And be forced to sit through

The desperate creation

Of a fantasy

Not meant to come true

C u in heaven

C u in heaven

U've given me something 2 die 4

U must have looked in 2 my soul and realized that it was cold

That it needed your radiant glow

Because 4 a long time I yearned 4 another soul

But why u went 4 this fool, I'll never know

After all, I'm not perfect

But in u I saw perfection

And I'm not all that smart

But u gave me wisdom

And I'm thankful that all my free time was devoted 2 u

And although I may have lost u

I will have eternity 2 search 4 u

C u in heaven

Parts of me die every day

Parts of me die every day

I just hope you manage to catch me

While there's still something left

The last time I spoke to you

The last time I spoke to you

I did it without mouthing words

I ran my hand across your photo

And said "I miss you"

As the tears began to flow

Too beautiful

You are too beautiful for me

I can't even make eye contact

Let alone speak

My ill-fated attempts

Resulting in nothing short of
great travesties

With quivering in-between

Your soul outshines even the
most

Brightest of spirits

It is the only light I wish

To guide my way

And your presence

Is nothing short of benevolent

It is a leading factor in why

I remain so driven

But alas, I was not made for
it

As if you are of a higher
power

And I am your witness

In mere servitude of it

You need someone more
accustomed to it

But you will always be

So beautiful to me

The endless road

I sometimes wonder if I am meant to die alone

My mission has always been to search the endless road

For another soul to call my own

But I find that this road often winds and turns

And I become lost

Amongst the endless trails,

Never able to find my way back

Each path turning to glass,

My very presence causing them to shatter

As I walk by

Making sure I never go the same way twice

And as I look behind,

I see all the faces, I had hoped to see by my side,

Start to slowly fade away

And shatter

Becoming my only proof of moving forward

As a new path begins to form

Untitled

I get what you are going
through

But I struggle analyzing it in
a way

That makes sense for my
brain to be able to

Articulate that knowledge
accurately

I see vivid pictures of your
pain

When I close my eyes

But still

It doesn't quite register with
me

How I should approach

Or how to consolidate you

So, I often just make things
worse

By giving ill advice

That could only possibly suit

A pale imitation of what you
are

Going through

To you, I appear illiterate in
knowing your pain

When there's so much, I wish
to say

But the words are all tangled
up

I just hope you know

I would not have these
thoughts

Had I not cared at all

Untitled

Does anything really matter?

Everything ends in grief

My whole family is
self-destructing

And emotions are secondary
to how they are

Perceived

I can't sleep

I have nightmares every time

I dream

I'm in pain

And on the verge of breaking

But what does that change?

I have no final say in things

I can only hope that
everything

I did was not in vain

That you saw, I truly tried

Even if it was in my own
broken way

And when I die,

I wonder what awaits me

Heaven or hell

Or somewhere In-between

I just hope whatever it is

Will allow you to have access

To my dreams

Because in life

There were so many things

That I had hoped for you to
see

Debra

Beauty

As it is

In your aspect

Likens to that of

The mellowing of candlelight

In that, the nature of your

Angelic eyes

Provide the basis for sight

Blind traversal is a given otherwise

You are as if wounds subsided

But to a lesser degree

In that as long as there is a fighting chance

Hope for the future

And a better tomorrow

Remain ever so prevalent

You are by definition

perfect

Getting older

life goes by in the blink of an eye

Beautiful and brief followed by heaven's sleep

If you blink you might miss it

Once so young, reckless, and full of blank pages

Now so old, wise, and full of stories

Life's too short to have regrets, you must learn to forgive and forget

Especially yourself

You have to live life to the fullest and conquer your dreams

For you only have one chance to see ends meet

Though it may seem pointless at first

It's only a test, there's more to come

Before your last breath

Before your body falls into an endless sleep

And your spirit goes to heaven

Carve your legacy

For your legacy can't die

It can only be carried on

Families will be united, and generations carried on

While we're all gone from the physical form

Awaiting to be reborn

The golden country – inspired by 1984

In my dreams

I witness unattainable beauty

A golden landscape that stretches

As far as the eye can see

With bits of what could be

Mankind's potential humanity

Cascaded amongst the blades of grass

That sway so majestically in the breeze

Igniting the trees

Setting them ablaze

And transferring onto me the flame

And through clutched fists

I denounce any ramifications

Of our past tyranny

As we blaze a path towards

A functional society

A dodged bullet

You have to show the right side

Or people will pass you by

Life is constantly moving

And so, no one cares whether you

Share it with them or not

It doesn't matter how hard you try

If you don't live up to expectations,

There is no redemption

Eventually, someone will nail it first try

And you'll be just a distant memory

If you are lucky

But chances are you'll be

That conversation starter

They bring up with friends

Whenever they reminisce about

How they dodged a bullet

Before I pushed you away

I hope in the afterlife

We get the chance to look through

Each other's eyes

And you can truly see

The real me

The plague

I feel like every day is a test

Because every day nothing seems to go our way

Every day we seem to lose someone that we thought was meant to
stay

And for every good person that leaves

A fake one takes their place

And it's starting to get overcrowded

Oversaturated by this poison leaking out

That can't be contained

Turning all my closest friends into slaves

Followers of this plague

Forcing them to cut me off

And leave me for someone birthed from the plague

Someone that would never do the same

But decide to walk with them anyway

Despite barely knowing their name

And now they are both carriers of the plague

I'm a man?

18

I'm a man?

I feel the same as I always have

A little mentally damaged

But still,

The same personality

And all my traits

I haven't transcended to a new plane

I even still sit here

And count the days

As if I am not 18 already

Is this just societies way of

Saying I'm ready?

Teens

It's astonishing to me how amazed

People are

Of the simplest things

Accomplished by teens

As if the worlds complex ways

Somehow make us less than capable

I'm not a genius

I'm just doing what I was

Meant to do

Untitled

I wonder if we never brought attention to anything

Whether or not nature would favor us kindly

To stand on the sidelines and see

If we will be our own downfall

Isn't it a shame we'd have to wait in the presence of

Looming uncertainty, knowing what is at stake?

Or do we see this as somehow

Being beneficial to the greater majority?

The prospect of potentially cutting loose

And discarding those last few parts of us

Have we no value?

When will we recognize us as human beings,

When as much as we stab each other,

Don't we see that we bleed?

How ignorant are we?

Is it simply an impossibility

For us to exist simultaneously?

Why is it that we can't show ourselves a little peace?

What is it that we are all afraid of?

When my grandpa died

When my grandpa died

I'm 17

Realizing I have a long journey ahead of me

A lot to do

A lot to see

Before I too

Am able to achieve this peace

And this is something that although sad

Gives me a better appreciation

And perception

Of what we truly have

I could go on and on about the pain

But all it takes is just a second

To step back and see

That this is only temporary

And for me to be sad

We would have had to meet

And so, it gives me comfort knowing

His presence will always be here with me

The conclusion

The message I sent

Was indicative

Of a response

Unwarranted

Unwavering silence

Following

An otherwise

Pleasant interaction

Our conversation was

Predisposed to ending

It was obvious based on

Your previous comment

But I had to go and ruin

The conclusion

Aesthetics

What is the purpose of aesthetics in a relationship

Other than to distract the two people involved

From the lack of compatibility between each soul?

Serving as compensation,

As if they can somehow rectify all the wrongs

As if him being tall

Can somehow justify him leaving you all alone

And being emotionally unavailable

When you need him the most

Not even bothering to return your calls

And meanwhile,

He thinks of you little

Because you happen to be small

Thinking that you are not able to do anything

On your own

Your pretty face being the only thing

That is keeping him there at all

Meanwhile,

Your soulmate is feeling lost

Sellout

Sometimes,

I feel like a sellout

Am I naturally inclined

To be this kind of person?

Or do I just gravitate

Towards something

I find more appealing?

Who would I be

Without any

Outside influences?

Who am I really?

Self-reliant

You need to be your own happiness

You can't expect others

To be it for you

The truth

The truth can be overwhelming

If told directly

So, bit by bit it must be

Spoken carefully

If we are to avoid

Hurting those indirectly

For one false slip of the tongue

Can be devastating to those

If not handled correctly

Becoming a weapon only never used directly

Some days

Some days

It's hard to keep going

When the world is in as bad of shape as it is

It leaves me unmotivated

In the pursuit of

My life's goals

My morality is constantly tested

And pushed beyond its limits

Who was I before all this?

Society

Sometimes, I feel absolutely appalled

When I think about life

And how so many people allow the influences

Of society

To embed itself within their minds

Causing them to judge each other

Based on characteristics that they think they like

All of which society has projected into their minds

Giving them the false belief that what they are doing

Is somehow right

How it is meant to be

But in reality, all they achieve

Is relinquishing themselves of

The ability to think free

Trading to be in sync with

Society's beliefs

Am I afraid?

One of the scariest realizations I had

Was when I looked into the mirror

Then slowly towards my hands

Clenching them tightly

As I examined in detail

The control I had

Realizing that what I possessed

Was something only temporary

For as long as I had breath

So, I started to wonder to myself:

Am I afraid of death?

Nothing's changed

Every day we act like

Nothing's changed

As we continue to drift

Further and further apart

An eye's clear view

Life can appear quite bland

If looked at directly from the
naked eye

Because it appears we are all
just

Wandering blindly,

Mindlessly chasing
objectives

Until we die

But upon closer examination,

There is immense beauty

That you can find

Woven between each and
every crevice

Of an individual's mind

Because we are so different

Yet one in the same

And this is despite having no

Collective identity

To maintain

Just different stories

And interpretations

To help develop our frames

We have been truly blessed
with the gift

Of being bearers of our own
names

Selfish

It sounds selfish

But I wish

The way I felt

Was all it took

For me and you

To be together

In the womb

At that moment in-between places

I wished for time to be accelerated

Because with every jostling motion,

Came a sudden reduction

My lifeline wrapped tightly

Cutting off my self-expulsion

Restricting the breath, it had once given me,

And replacing it with solemn dreams of peace

But still through this insanity

My soul wanted to find a place to be

So, with the helping hand of a miracle

Allowing me to be free

He made it so I may breathe

D.O.B March 29th, 2004

Your reasoning

It's hard for me not to question

Your reasoning

But I wonder if there's more to this

Whole just being friends thing

You love me enough

To not want to risk losing me

So, do I place that higher than

You not being compelled

To want to risk everything?

I don't know

All I know is

There's nothing in this world

I wouldn't do for you

Clarity

I wish I could achieve such a level of clarity

That nothing in this world could faze me

I am aware of all potential dangers and outcomes already

And all of life and its secrets now flow through me

Steadily

I have felt this feeling

But only momentarily

And in that moment

Depression and anxiety

The things that have always chased me

Now were the ones that breathed heavy

And all the self-hatred

I have always manifested—

Gone

I could see so clearly

My life for once was right in front of me

Until I got that jolt

That brought me back to reality

Not hard to see

It's not hard to see

Where things went wrong

I knew it from the moment we met

That you were the type of person

I wanted to spend my life with

It wasn't love at first sight

But rather love at first interaction

It only took those first few words

For me to know you were special

But I knew I was going into it broke

Because outside of that moment

My life wasn't worth much

How could I possibly afford another?

I should have seen it coming

Although it hurt at first

I was willing to settle as friends

If it still gave me a part in your life

The reason we die

I wonder if the reason we die

Is to see ourselves from another side

In the form of new bodies

Looking down on our past lives

Our essence transferred to an empty frame

Wiped clean of remembrance

And granted

A new name

And a new face

All for the sake of continuing the chain

But what does it all mean?

And what's the point if we can't remember our past names

And all the lessons we learned along the way?

How can we break free

From the never-ending cycle we are caught between?

Your posts

When I see you post pictures of him,

I tell myself I don't care anymore

As if false statements can distract me

From how I really feel

Another part of a messed-up game

Another part of a messed-up game

Another part of a messed-up game

If deep in your heart, you
knew

How much I loved you

It would have put to rest any
doubts you had

About my love being true

It would have told you, you
could trust me

When you really needed
someone to

And in terms of separation

There would have been no
need as I was with you

But with love being true

It can be hard to prove

When so many people are
constantly using you

And in you I knew this was
true

Because nothing I ever said
or did could convince you

But maybe if you knew

What I had been through

How I was scared and
confused

You could have seen I was on
a mission to prove

That no matter how damaged
I could still love you

I tried so hard

And never had the intention
of breaking your heart

But to you, I guess it was all
the same

I was just there to play
another part in some
messed-up game

Your aura

I can hear when you speak

But I can't seem to ever listen

As soon as you are within my peripheral vision

Your aura diverts my attention

And everything you say

Is heavily filtered

Coming through as

Indecipherable audio

I have yet to

Move past

That initial stage of being

In complete awe of you

Heaven

As I drift to sleep, I dream of
a magic place

A place where I will see my
lost friends

And remnants of what
could've been

A place free of sin

A paradise

Beyond the golden gates lies
a city of angels in the sky

Peace and harmony

A soft gentle breeze and
cherry trees

A place where lost souls are
found

Old people are young

And peace and love are
unbound

As I walk through the golden
gates immediate peace is felt

The soft gentle breeze
soothes the soul

The cherry blossoms calm the
nerves

And the sun glistens off the
pearly white robes

This is heaven I can feel it

I can feel a strong presence

A man of the holy spirit

He says his name is Jesus

His voice soft as silk

As calm as a gentle breeze

He tells me it's not my time
yet and that he's proud of me

I hear beeping and voices as I
start to fade in

I wake up in a hospital bed

The surgeon said he thought
he lost me, I flatlined

When love finds me

When love finds me

I hope it's in the presence

Of my own company

I would hate to be reliant on others

For such a basic necessity

Obscurity

I wish I could gift something that holds its value

For eternity

But most things just fade into obscurity

Pain

I used to think my pain

Was unique only to me

That no one else could possibly understand

What I was going through

It was incomprehensible to me that

Another person

Had experienced what I had

Since we are all such unique beings

A strange light

I thought it was a star that
flew by

The bright light in the sky

However,

It stopped dead in its tracks
and hovered nearby

The bright light piercing the
sky

I felt like I was going blind

Its shining radiant glow

It let out a low cry

A piercing tone

Like it was distressed almost

I felt its gaze upon me

Like it wanted something of
me

It began moving slowly
across the sky

Still fixed on me

It wanted me to follow it

So, I gave chase

I felt like I was running a
maze

It took me through the alleys
and the streets

Until eventually through a
cemetery

Where it beamed around
among the graves

Until eventually its light
shined on one

A little girl, only a year old

Funny how that works

Love taught me how to deal with pain

Pain taught me how to love

It's funny how that works

The start of every journey

Upon my conception into this world

I was a blank slate

Filled with too much envy to explore

Because the generation before did not bother to explain to me

The rules I would need

In order to make sense of the journey

I was to endure

The lessons they obtained

Locked behind the same layer of disdain

I first felt upon my entrance to this new place

And so bit by bit

It was up to me

To obtain the same lessons

Already graced by others in my same place

And so, to this day

I still swear

Every generation starts off as a blank slate

Back together

I showed you all the broken parts of me

With the hope that you would help me

Put myself back together

I didn't mean to drive you away

The mystique of jinx

To refer to simultaneous speech simply as a jinx,

Diminishes any mystique that it may bring

Perhaps we all walk around with a piece of God in us each

Allowing us to operate individually as beings

But every now and then,

We must sync

If we wish to prolong this dream

What if death is simply a side effect after having reached

Maximum fatigue

And a temporary sleep is needed

To refresh each piece

Which is then in return

Reintroduced as a new being

The only consequence being

Maybe we have all been separated for too long

Anger

The things you do out of anger

Can have a profound and lasting impact

Why risk causing permanent damage

Because of something that is only momentary?

Love made you hate me

If loving you is what made you hate me,

Then I wish you luck

With the one that puts in

Half the effort

Desert island

Your eyes used to be like the ocean

And I would be lost at sea

But now I can't imagine myself

Anywhere else

But stranded

On a desert island

The line

I wonder who will take my place

And exchange with me

My age for their youth

Knowing as soon as they do,

A curse will linger over

And haunt them until their time is due

Because

There is high demand for this thing we call life

And unless you know how to play it just right

You may find yourself at the back of the line

Trading spots sooner than you may like

What is this existence?

What is this existence?

We are conscious to a certain
extent

But is this really
consciousness?

It seems we have always
been programmed

With certain desires

And requirements

But it's so deep

We've never really
questioned it

Is this really free thinking?

Or is this just code being fed
into our heads?

And we are really this
oblivious to it

Because why else would we
create for ourselves

Such limits?

Are we just a flawed system?

When all others are just
programs

We can either swap out and
tinker with

Until we get it right

Or keep and suffer with

Until somethings fails

And we wonder why our
systems never align

When we die

When we die,

I hope you no longer associate me

With the mistakes of my earthly form

I hope you acknowledge that

We've become something more

A fading light

You still call it love

After you've fought so hard to keep it

As if all the times they have tried to slip away

Have done nothing to warrant a change

Still trying to hold on tight

As if you are trying to suffocate

The very atoms occupying the empty space

Because physically you don't seem to notice the change

But mentally they have already escaped

And now you are left

Trying to hold on tight

To what is left

Of a fading light

Space

Only the empty space

Knows how often

I think of you

Untitled

I wish I could reciprocate

The feelings you give to me

But I lack anything of value

To offer you

Just my way of thinking

And point of view

But I don't feel like that means a whole lot

When there are others out there

Just as capable

With a whole lot more to bring to the table

And since this is all I'm brining

And I've already made so many mistakes,

There's not a whole lot worth holding on to

Still, I hope one day you decide

I'm worth giving a chance

The difference

The difference between me and you is that

You could have nothing

And I would still want to be with you

For you being you

Please wipe your feet before coming in

Please wipe your feet at the door

Before you come in

I've had too many

Enter with dirt unseen

Only to merely pass through

And leave what was once clean

Filled with dirt and debris

So, I ask that

If you here merely to visit

Please avoid touching items sacred

Because they are easily damaged

And if you wish to remain for a long stay

To let your presence be known

As someone that can maintain this home

Your place

Your place was already carved out

Long before you came along

But I was too preoccupied with the anticipation

Of your arrival

To recognize earlier on

Our introduction had to be put on hold

While I made some mistakes

And learned some lessons

So, I could be prepared for the day

Our meeting finally took place

Idols

The more people I idolize

That pass away

The more I start to become comfortable

With the idea of death too

Am I supposed to be at peace here?

Why would God let me feel so oppressed

If I had a full life ahead of me?

Is my time here only meant to be spent briefly,

To see how all this is meant to be?

I'm equipped with the bare minimum necessities

To observe and experience basic interaction

Nothing is ever long lasting

So, I have nothing to drive my ambitions

My experiences serve as vague recreations of a bigger picture

Never fully explored in depth

Just simply observed from afar

Am I supposed to be happy

And at peace here?

The world

Until I come to terms with the world

And what it wants

I will continue to live in exile

While everyone else grows

Untitled

In all the times I've spent

Consumed by the darkest nights,

It was thoughts of you

That allowed to shine through the brightest light

Repairing my heart once cracked and torn

And causing it to be reborn

The light gleaming through the crevices

Causing my cold heart to grow warm

And allowing my mind to ease

Searching for dreams

It so adored

Because if it weren't for you

And the light you let shine through

My heart would never have known true beauty

When I look at you

Wired differently

What truly separates us from being one?

We are all just as capable as the next

But something in each of us

Is wired different

For instance, my brain seems to forget everything

When it comes to you

I sometimes say and do things

I wouldn't otherwise do

I sometimes stutter

And even say things that come off as confusing

And I wonder if any of this

Takes away from me as an individual

Because after all, I am still that same

Loving, thoughtful person

But I wonder if these outward presentations

Ultimately affect how you see me

I wish I could get to the root of this

So, you could see the true intentions

I try so hard to be perceived

Mental health

Mental health

Struggling with mental health

Is a showing of resilience

Keep going

Even when the days feel like

They're blending together

Time

I'm still hoping time was just a little late

Reserving a space

And has already made note

Of the arrangements needed

For me to once again

See your face

Times I'm afraid

There are times I'm afraid

I'm going to lose you

My mind starts racing

And all I can think about

Are all the mistakes I've made

The mess I've put you through

But then I remember

All the times I've made you smile, hugged, and laughed with you

And deep down I know everything will be ok

Because whenever I am feeling worried

You always show up unexpectedly

And make my whole day

After we die

I go through life

Writing down all the ways

I messed up with you

With the hope that

After we die

We'll be able to sit down

And properly discuss everything

Much of life is situational

It was through you I learned

That much of life is purely situational

That the outcome is largely dependent on the circumstance

I saw this when

After he caught your eye

You let him walk all over you

When he made it quite clear from the beginning

How little you really meant to him

How despite all the times he fought and argued with you

You always countered it by showing nothing but love back

And when he left you begged him to come back

I watched how a person could put it all up front

And then be rewarded for it

I watched how that boy slipped you that note

Just so on your way out you could toss it in the trash

That same boy who had stayed up night and day

Rehearsing what he had hoped to say

Only to write it down in the end

In the eyes of a stranger

There's a kind of beauty

In the eyes of a stranger

A fresh new gaze

Witness free of past mistakes

In a way you get to start from scratch

With the chance to be the person

You have always wanted to be

No need to worry anymore about the what if's

And the could have been's

You have been given a clean slate

To build on from lessons previously learned

To create new memories

And loosen old weight

Maybe this will be the time

I finally learn from previous mistakes

Toxic

We are all capable of being toxic

But you chose not to acknowledge it

Instead, it was easier for you to move on to the next

And say I was the cause of it

Forgetting the role you played in it

I'm still mad at myself for the way I acted

During those moments

But you don't lose any sleep over it

As far as you are concerned,

I'm just another lover gone rogue

Another name on a long list of men

Undeserving of your affection

Expendable soldiers fighting your war

Grew apart

She hates me

But still every day

I wish she were with me

From the beginning, I thought he would always be with me

But somewhere along the line

We grew apart

And one day,

He did not wish to see me

But maybe I'm just talking silly

Ignoring what she did to me

What he put me through

But that's when I realized

We are in parallels of one truth

Because I guess when I left

So, did you

Like a flame

I wish to go out

With regal grace

How you think

If everyone could see how you think

Maybe they would be more capable

Of making their own conscious decisions

On how they feel about you personally

Instead of having to rely on others

To do it for them

Unison

I have never quite understood this phenomenon

One experiences

When their heart is so enamored

By another person's presence

Because it's a feeling that dwarfs all others

In comparison

And all you really hope for

Is for their heart and yours

To be in unison

Because at that moment

Everyone else falls short in comparison

And to be with anyone else

You cannot imagine

Because this feeling feels heaven sent

But in all my years I have never borne witness to anyone

Achieve this unison

I needed depression

I needed depression

To help achieve my goals

But I may have sunk deeper

Than I intended

Sorry

I wish I could think of something else

Other than "Sorry"

For everything that I've done

It has little meaning

In a world that moves so fast

Their initial view

As involuntary as it may be

Still, I struggle

With my constant worrying

And low self-esteem

And how that behavior is influencing

The way I am perceived

Because I jump headfirst into everything

As if I have to or I will never get the opportunity

But all I really achieve is

Painting a picture

That others can't quite see

And so, they interpret it differently

And now I am perceived as being the enemy

But despite my actions being misconstrued

I make no effort to change people's view

Instead, I choose to suffer for it

Because I believe their initial view

To be true

Innocence

It has been a while since I sat

And just adored the fact you
are in my life

It wasn't too long ago that I
had a persistent stay

Upon the epitome of
innocence

Where on each day fallen

It was to constructs of you
forming

Upon the very basis of your
essence

To dream would mean to be
greeted by your
manifestations

But to awaken

That would mean to
experience

That dreaded jolt of
realization

On which to be the onset of
an even worse ratification

The recollection of the petty
mistakes I've made

But in doing so,

I hope to have reassured your
mind

On the migration towards
something better

I hear you are with another

I wish you and him the best

He is lucky to be able to

Wake up to you each morning

And although I used to think
of the long silences,

As something to gripe about

Now I just look at it as
confirmation

You are being treated right

Still, your beauty guides me
through

Each and every day

Everything has fallen into
place as it

Should have been

See you in heaven

My own bed

Being left alone with my thoughts

Has made sure my nights are never pleasant

There's nothing I want more

Than to be able to

Sleep soundly in my own bed

My dreams

My dreams come alive

When you're involved

The one I loved

The one I loved

Isn't the one I ended up with

But I still search for them

In everyone else

The chase

Why must my heart always dive headfirst

Into a raging storm,

Knowing it has been lied to before?

And only seems to grieve when the door is open no more

So many times, it has told me "I've never felt this way before"

But it has always been to a closed door

And every time there was an open door

It chose to ignore

Seemingly because it enjoyed the chase more

But every time there was a new chase to explore

It always led to a closed door

And my heart would feel weighed down even more

Like it was missing something from its core

And it always had me feeling like I could love no more

Until the day my heart found her

And wanted to no longer chase storms

Unintelligent

They say we learn from our mistakes

So, I must be rather unintelligent

Because I don't seem to learn

Until it's too late

My mind operates on loss

So, I'll have to lose you

To make a positive change in the end

I cannot be anything less than

The monster

You now envision

Conscious

If we were truly conscious

Our consciousness would surpass

What limited knowledge is available to us

And when faced with a choice,

There would be no need to

Deliberate

Because regardless of the fact

Whatever we choose,

Would have been right all along

My hardest hurdle

I wish every time I thought of you

Was the last time

It would not only be

The perpetual victory of me

Overcoming the hardest hurdle I've ever had to

But it would also be the compromise that satiates

The part of me that still loves you

The road shown

The road shown

Is both a blessing

And an opportunity to behold

For had my mother not pulled me to the side

To show me where things went wrong

I would have taken the same road

The hardest thing

The hardest thing you can do is

Come to terms with being alone

When your heart wants

Nothing more than love

Peace

Sometimes I cry

Not because I am sad

But because I want to feel the sensation

Of releasing every emotion that I had

And watch as they run down my face in the form of a stream

Where my pent-up frustration and broken dreams

Can finally be free

Taking on new meaning

As they run downstream

Finally bringing peace to my dreams

Pain

If nothing more

I deserve this pain

T.O.D

While lying in bed

I watch as the rain drizzles down the window

And I am immediately overcome with sorrow

Upon realizing

That with every drop gone by

I start to feel weaker

As I approach my inevitable demise

The beeping of the machine

In rhythm with my falling heartbeat

Slower and slower

The lines creep across the screen

Until eventually the beeping starts to overshadow the rain

And suddenly

I feel as if I'm not on the same plane

No longer in sync with my being

As I hop out from my capsule

In time to hear my T.O.D

Alone

Every day I try to convince myself

I've told the world enough

I've let my presence be known

But no amount of shouting

Makes me feel any less alone

Wilted flowers

You gave me a garden

From which I was able to pick out a bouquet

But one by one

The flowers began to wilt and shrivel away

You must have planted the seeds too deep though

Because long after you were gone

I found myself still returning to this place

A lingering portion of me still wishing you had stayed

But in your absence

I found that, that single bouquet

Now paled in comparison

To the acres of land that now flourished

Since you have been away

Happier

The suffering will be great

But I think if I assassinate my character

I can help push you towards someone

That makes you happier

Among darkness

Only when I'm alone,

At the mercy of darkness,

Am I able to see the light

That my soul so desperately needs

And only while in its presence

Do I truly feel at peace,

Able to freely breathe

And let my mind run free

While I lay stretched out

Among my sheets

Every breath taken in

Feeling like fresh relief

But alas this never lasts long

Because before you know it

I see an amber glow

As I glance towards the window

Pushed away

I know that I've already

Pushed you away

But every now and then

I'll have moments where I return to

The old me

I just wish you were still here to see it

Immortality

Immortality

Immortality

There is no greater gift

Than what remains of you

After death

With every December

With every December

Comes thoughts of January

And the coming days

But with February now approaching,

The anticipation begins mounting

By June, reality has started to settle in

And come next December,

We are ready to start again

A hostage personality

I find myself drifting off

Unto parallels

In an effort to gain sentience

And become independent from ones

True self

But my mind is like books on a shelf

And no matter what

The building blocks are always there

To keep me grounded

And stuck in place

Never isolated from where I originate

I find myself drifting off

Unto parallels

When freedom calls

When freedom calls

I hope we will be there to listen

Because we would have had to become

Members of the voiceless

For us to truly bring to us

Its attention

Love used to be carefree

Love used to be young

And carefree

Blue was my favorite color

And 6 months was an eternity

It wasn't until I met you

That love began to show its age

Red became a substitute for blue

And I was just lucky enough to not have

Any noticeable bruises

6 months could not have come

Fast enough

The mirror

I failed to see that

When I tried so hard for you to like me,

I acted as a mirror

And reflected everything you did

Right back to you

Never allowing us to grow as individuals

And after a while, it got harder for you

To differentiate between the two

I got lost in the reflection

And no longer knew who I was

When you looked at me

All you could see was you

And not wanting to have to get by solely

On self-love

We began to drift away

You could no longer look into a mirror

Chemical manipulation

I hate having to be medicated

Just to exist

Knowing that happiness

Is not a feeling I often experience

Absent of chemical manipulation

Who would have thought that I'd need assistance

For such basic function

How can I obtain true happiness?

My book of life

Upon coming home

And removing my coat

I first seek the company

Of my dimly lit room

Where on the table

In front of the soft
candlelight

Lies

The book of my life

And every now and then

While in its presence

I must sit down

And allow myself to go blind

While the lord guides my
hand

Through every line

But through his divine will

Has allowed for every line
only to define

Never letting the origin of
each entry obtained

Destroy

Leaving my heart stained

Instead allowing it to
strengthen

And bind together each page

What we've been through

Sometimes,

I find myself disregarding the things we've been through

I act as if I deserve more than what's being shown

As if I can somehow disregard the pain I've inflicted

Blind to my mistakes

I continue to act as if nothing's changed

But a lot has

And I can see that in your subtleties

You've been helping me put on a façade

That everything is ok

That I've been granted a clean slate

But the cracks are beginning to show

And now I'm afraid of losing you

Untitled

Every time our relationship marginally improves

I feel bad for discovering something new

I could have been doing for you

When we first met

I promised myself I would do nothing but the best for you

But I feel like I break that promise every time

I realize there's more I could do

I find myself

Reminiscing on the past year

And I realize that

I've only ever been partly there

Slowly over a period of time,

Building up to where I am now

How can I foresee this growth

And be everything I could be at once?

The loudest voice

The loudest voice is often the one that goes unheard

The voice is full of strength and speaks powerful words

But what good are those words if they are not heard?

What good are they if they are not on a pedestal?

So, everyone can soak in their gold

Their words have the potential to catch eyes

To influence people during this cold time

But life just passes them by

And their voice goes unheard

Becoming just a whisper in the wind

Words in a bottle

Lost at sea

Untitled

It's easy to treat people less than human

When you don't know them

But you start to realize how it was

Before those that you know now

Were eventually befriended

And suddenly I'm interested in knowing

Their stories

And how they landed on the same page as me

To begin with

I want to be able to accept them

Regardless of where they come from

Or their life choices

Because outward appearances are oftentimes deceptive

I want to believe strongly in my heart that

Their appearance has meaning

And that their words will flow nicely on a given page

But if not then

I'll just release a second edition

With the mistakes corrected

Is this love?

I didn't want to believe it at first

But I'd be lying if I told you

I was madly in love with you

The love I have for you

Isn't the kind I'm used to

It doesn't overwhelm me

To the point where I'm afraid to speak to you

I don't feel the need to overanalyze every syllable

There aren't constant explosions going off in the distance

Making me too afraid to be near you

Or swarms of butterflies every time your name comes to mind

Instead, there's a strange calmness

Is this what love is like?

Fake ignorance

If I didn't know about it

I wouldn't care about it

But now that I know about it

I care about it

Its that state of mind

We sometimes forget about

The results of never giving people the benefit of a doubt

But ignorance is not always an intention

Sometimes all that's needed

Is a little education

Untitled

I had hoped your soul

Felt at peace with mine the most

But in one swift move

We went from close

To distant

To independent

But I am not independently living

I drag thoughts of you with me

Through each and every day

Struggling to catch my breath underneath the immense weight

But to let go

Would mean to truly be alone

I envy you for being able to live your life

Each and every day

For me it is always the same

The mask

I wish I could have seen that you were wearing a mask

Because all this time I have been blindly traversing a path

I had laid out

Guided by projections of

What I thought was a possibility we could have

But I failed to see

That it was simply not reality

And that in all actuality

I had been unweaving the close-knit thread between us

And now its strained

And I cannot describe the pain I feel

Knowing I was the cause

I care about you more than anything

But I feel doomed to repeat the same mistakes

Among friends

Being among friends

Is a different kind of feeling

It's a temporary moment

Outside the realm of life's daily occurrences

A designated area of escape

So long as you remain within range

But because of where I'm currently at in life,

My reception has been a little spotty as of late

Untitled

I sometimes question if I am truly worthy of you

Because you are what I think of if there was ever a woman so true

But my heart refuses to pass you by

And I sometimes question why

Because I don't feel like I deserve a woman of your caliber

In my life

And my history of misery says I shouldn't even try

But still, you have yet to leave my mind

You are the first thing on it from the darkness of night

To every time I rise

And it makes me wonder why you even bothered to reply

I guess God really did know what I liked

The better part of not having it

Happiness is the thing I experience

To the better part of not having it

I want it

But each time I encounter it,

It is merely the predecessor

To a false sense of fulfillment

A rare occasion only experienced

Because of the slight release of pressure

From the buildup of everything inside

A false positive

Another body with flaws

I wish I could look at myself

As just another body with flaws

But I tend to look at myself deeper

And sift through the crevices

To get a clearer understanding of

All that is wrong

And what I find is that despite

All the times I truly try

It's as if I am not in complete control sometimes

My brain deciding on its own

How it will behave that day

And afterwards becoming upset

When things don't go its way

The whole world crumbling all around me

And I'm just along for the ride

While I watch as potential relationships

And friendships die

Words

Saying something is one thing

But what matters most

Is what those words mean to you

I can't recall who I was

I can't recall who I was

Before everything got so broken

A repressed memory lost in a convoluted maze

I've flip flopped between multiple personalities

I've changed the way I speak

And how I think

Unaware I was leaving pieces of myself scattered in the process

All in a bid to grow closer with those I thought I cared about

But in the end, none of them stuck around long enough

For me to rediscover things about myself

And now I'm left sifting through a backlog of memories

A year of healing

Despite what the calendar might say

The remnants of last year still remain

Although momentarily shielded by fireworks

And the new year cheer

Its ripples will continue to be felt

Throughout the year

Let this be a year of healing

And recovery

Can we really picture the inside of a man's mind?

Even if you really tried,

You could never picture the inside of a man's mind

Because even if you were given the chance to take a glance inside

And you saw something

You thought you should despise,

You would be letting your eyes be your guide

Instead of taking a second to truly figure out

And understand why

He felt this way inside

So, before you try

Why not just take a second to ask why?

And be that shoulder to lean on when he cries

Will we remain the same through peace?

I wonder in heaven

When we make our way through the gates

And we are met with a gentle breeze

And eternal peace

If we would still be who we are

Or if all that would cease

Because I've always thought the pain we experienced

Is what drove us to be unique

But if that was the case

Then it would mean my soul

Forever trying to cling to something

Already gone

So maybe through peace

There are more lessons to be learned

And the ones we have brought along with us

Can serve as the first stepping stones

Untitled

You have always had the key
to my heart

But that key is to remain
locked away

As I was blinded for too long

Scared at what might be the
outcome

If I were to share my hearts
song

But now I see that time did
not wait up for me

As you are now someone
else's key

And now all my heart can do
is beat for you endlessly

But I guess that's how it was
always meant to be

For you to be truly happy

And although I care about
you more than words can
express

God blessed another soul

Before mine could confess

But still, I will always be
here

For the beating will never
rest

And even though deep down
I wish I hadn't had waited for
so long

Maybe this was how it was
planned all along

To allow way

For his hearts song

Room 108

Through the peephole, I
could see room 108

The man showed up there at
the same time every night

A strange lengthy fellow

Barely visible in the dim light

Every night he just stood
there

He had on the same oversized
coat that darkened his face

A walking silhouette, a
shifting shape in the light

But as quickly as he had
appeared

He was gone

Every night it was like this

It concerned me a great deal

I knocked on 108 only to get
no answer

I spoke to the neighbors only
to be met with the same
response

"I've never seen him"

I thought I was losing my
mind

This decrepit building must
be messing with my head

But one night, things were
different

It was 1 am

I had been woken by the
sounds of sirens and
marching throughout the hall

The police had been called

They had been notified of a
foul smell coming from room
108

They knocked on the door
only to get no response

So, they walked in and called
out

Only to be greeted by the
same man lying motionless
on the floor

Dark coat and all

He had been dead for at least
a month

Self-centered

The problem with talking to someone

That's self-centered

Is that it doesn't matter how loud you speak

They only hear what they want to hear

Deathbed letter

I was so in love with you

To the point where

When I was at my lowest,

I had thoughts of being on my deathbed

Just so I could pour my soul into

A letter for you

Before I died

And in it would contain every moment

Where I felt I cold have done something different

Maybe even better

But I probably wouldn't be able to dwell on it for too long

As the only thing keeping me alive at that moment

Would be the thought that

Maybe you'll come to visit

Be at peace

Sometimes we just have to be at peace with the world

And accept the way things are

To come to terms with the impending battles

And the things that have the potential

To make them that much harder

Grant yourself acceptance

Whether or not the outcome is in your favor

Everything happens for a reason

And there's no point in fighting for something

Destined to escape

That one friend

I want to be that one friend that never leaves

No matter the trials and tribulations we face

But for me it has always seemed like its destiny

For people to leave

As if me being here

Only incentivizes

I will be questioning

That if I was the one to leave

Whether or not they too

Would be trying to hold on to me

So desperately

But I could never find it in me to do such a thing

So, I will continue to be that one friend

Others don't see

Life is like gold

The fact that we have limited time here

Is what makes life so unique

It's like gold

If gold was abundant, it would be worthless

If we lived forever,

Eventually life would become dull

Because at some point we would have achieved everything

And we'd have to watch those we love pass away

At that point, we'd wish for death

So, we could escape this eternal torment

Life would lose meaning

And we'd give up on trying

And eventually, when the stars and the sun go out,

We would be in space floating around aimlessly

The fact that we are able to die is a blessing

Even if sometimes it doesn't feel that way

I'm sure we all wish we could have a little more time though

Cursed

I wish I could see you more clearly

But instead, I'm blinded by my own insecurities

Maybe if I could love myself more

I could love you too

Although I'm prepared to do whatever it takes

God has cursed me with an unlovable face

And so too often do I have to deal with the consequences

That take its place

And since I'm cursed

My experiences are limited

I just flow through it all the same

I don't get upset anymore

When people call me ugly,

I don't get upset anymore

Or feel the need to hide my face

Instead, to me it's as simple as

Them just not being destined

To occupy the same space as me

Instead, I'm grateful for them announcing

Their departure

Before their arrival

It saves me the trouble

Masked pain

"Good things come to those that wait"

Is what he said to me

Even though he was the one in pain

I could tell because he would always refrain from being called

By his name

As if the slightest mention of it would cause others pain

He would rather remain a nameless face

Because he thought that if he wore a mask

Then others would think he was ok

But this only drew attention

And so, people began to look past his face

And focus their attention on where it should have been

In the first place

Highs and lows

My days consist of a series of highs and lows

Sometimes it's hard for me to differentiate

Between reality

And the things my mind tells me

Without warning, I take a dive into the past

Without a life jacket

Trying to stay afloat amongst the hopelessness and regret

I've forgotten how to swim

Rather I never knew how to

Instead, I force myself deeper into the abyss

As if drowning myself can somehow make up for it

But no matter how deep I go,

A sliver of myself always survives

To remind me that self-hatred

Is not the way to go

And I am pulled out before

I can reach the bottom

What else is there?

Despite knowing what death is,

I feel like I could die right now

And still live

Something inside me just fails to comprehend

The absence of consciousness

Its incomprehensible to me

How a being filled with so much life

Can just one day cease to exist

What else is there besides this?

I never wanted to be this person

I never had any intentions of being this person

But you get so caught up in being

What they think you should be

That you forget about the person

You are meant to be

What made them pain me

As anything other than myself

And my true intentions?

How can I convey to them

The person I truly am

When they've already given in so deeply to

Their own flawed interpretations?

After all,

By giving in, I've made their perceptions a reality

And have reassured them

That they will be getting paid the commission

For their artwork

Hunted

I saw a bright light move past
as I lowered the blinds

A flicker of light shining
throughout the house

Igniting the room

Followed shortly by a
blood-curdling scream

A loud cry heard in the night

Sending birds perched in the
trees scattering

Their squawks echoing

The light dissipated only for
a moment

Before returning more hectic

A jostling motion

Sending beams of light
scattering wildly in the night

Lighting up the forest and
exposing the trees

The sounds of footsteps heard
as it drew closer

Amplified by the twigs and
leaves

With staggers in-between

Short pauses

The sounds drew closer and
closer

The light brighter

Until eventually I saw him

A man

Emerging from the trees

At least what was left of one

Sometimes I feel defeated

Sometimes I feel defeated

Sometimes I feel defeated

Sometimes I feel defeated

And unsure of what to do

My past mistakes continue to manifest themselves

In those new

And time is anything but idol

In the moments I spend assessing the damage

Desperately trying to make amends

But I know it will probably end up like this again

I am not really this type of person

But around you

My brain fails to retain this information

And me and you are always stuck between

Standing and falling

I already miss this

I already miss this

Despite our interactions being present

As if you are a long missed soul

That has previously graced me with their presence

And now I have finally caught up to you

And said what I was meant to

Now, if you leave

I will not regret anything

My journey is complete

The scars of my journey

Sometimes I may face despair

But it's times like those where I am reminded

That I like to breathe air

After all, cold steel and flesh don't mix

And every time I press that knife against my skin

I am reminded of this

I don't look at the everlasting scars as something I should hide

Nor fear as something I will be judged by

Instead, I like to show them off as

Lasting impressions of the journey I survived

And showcase all the fights I've won on the inside

The same war

Why do people think being black is so wrong?

If God did not want us to exist

All he would have to do is snap his fingers

And that would be it

We would be nothing but dust in the wind

A forgotten sin

But yet we are still here

Fighting the same war we always have

To no end

Trying to spread the message of people being

Comfortable in their own skin

We fight not just for us

But our fallen brothers and sisters as well

And although we cannot make them reappear

We will fight for them for as long as we are still up here

When I'm no longer here

When I take my last breath

And shed my last tear

I hope that in the event of me no longer being here

What I lived and died for

Would have been made clear

Because when I was alive no one seemed to care

Only when we die

Do people seem to grow ears

I don't have an anchor

I don't have anyone to act as an anchor

And show me what love is

So how am I supposed to be happy here

And love myself

When everyone makes a spectacle of my flaws?

My actions and decision making

Become less graceful every day

I no longer have the strength to give it my all

I am merely doing the bare minimum to get by

I retreat back into the darkness

And through my clouded lens,

There's no sign of a bright sky

How I feel within

I want to communicate how she makes me feel within

But I can't seem to find the words to begin

I haven't said anything

But already I am fighting myself to let her take a glance in

To tell her how she lit the burning fire

That burned to no end

And how every time I thought of her

I could see the flame growing from within

I know what my heart desires

But I'm afraid that if I let her know

It will put out the fire

Unpaid actors

My whole family

Is full of unpaid actors

Trying desperately

To make it in Hollywood

Skeletons

We are all skeletons playing dress-up

I just got stuck with the last costume

I'm proud of myself

Whenever I feel like ending it,

I remind myself that

I only have one life to live

So, I might as well see this thing out

I should stop beating myself down

Because I have a habit of measuring myself

Based on others success

Everyone's path is different

And sure, I've made a lot of mistakes in my life

But who hasn't?

I can say now that I'm proud of myself

For lasting as long as I have

Not willing

The ones that despise this generation

Are the ones unwilling to teach it

Loneliness

Loneliness isn't when the love you have for me

No longer exists

It's when despite all of it

I still put you above the rest

Today

Today love came in the form of a song

I wanted to send it to you

But I remembered

You had already moved on

Why do good people die?

Why do so many good people have to die?

And how come the ones that killed them are still alive?

Some say that God needed them to come home

That he needs good people to save everyone's souls

But others say that the world is just cold

Good people suffer and bad people prosper

People coerced into becoming monsters

This is the devils work

Hell is on earth

People seduced into becoming followers of his cult

Forced to do his dirty work

Different wars being raised on earth

Different ideologies being birthed

And meanwhile, good souls continue to leave earth

God's soldiers

Egotistical

I guess I was egotistical for thinking

You would respond to my messages

Or answer my calls

I wish I was different

I wish I was different in the sense that

I was someone you thought was worth

Giving a chance

But I'm not so

What else can I do but

Be made to go through these changes?

With the hope that once I'm fixed

It will somehow improve my chances

Foundation

I hate the thought of having

To fall in love with someone

That isn't you

I don't want to new make memories

Using the foundation

A house was supposed to be built on

With you

Waiting in anticipation

I don't think I'm ever truly living in the moment

Because I'm always waiting in anticipation for something

It seems like every day is just filler for another day

Because I'm always waiting impatiently

For something to come my way

I start to feel like a slave as I wait

Watching impatiently as time slips away

And in this state

My mind starts to lust over

Something not obtainable within this hour

This state leaving me

Susceptible to outside forces

While my mind is coercing with chaotic voices

Becoming unaware of time

As I wait

Trapped in my own mind

Fiending for a chance to leave

My present behind

I wish you could love the real me

But instead, I'm stuck auditioning

For a movie, I'm not guaranteed

A role in

A whole world

If it wasn't for you

My mind would have no place

To escape to

As soon as I see your name pop up

On my phone

A whole world is created inside my brain

With me and you

At the center of it all

Stranded

All your forevers left me stranded in the past

Unable to move on

I guess it really was forever

All your forevers left me stranded in the past

To your convenience

You love me

When it's to your convenience

What does your love even mean

When you treat it as little more than

A superficial bargaining chip?

Something you resort to

In a last-ditch effort

To win over my affection

And its working

Forever

Forever is a lot shorter than I remember

But maybe it's still going

Despite this hiatus

And we'll run into each other again

When were a bit older

And a lot wiser

That way we can pick up where

This forever thing left us

My love

I was made to feel like my love

Could never amount to you

No matter how hard I tried,

The execution was not justifiable

To the absolute spectacle

That was you

Nothing I ever did even came close to

Expressing it the way I wanted to

And now I'm left to wonder

If there was something more

I could have done

So much better

I don't like coffee

But I don't mind drinking it with you

I don't watch that show

But maybe it's something I can get into

I don't like that song

But I'll listen along

And I didn't like that movie

The first time around

But with you

It was the greatest thing I ever saw

My point is

You make everything so much better

The park

When rain begins to pour

Igniting a raging storm

It harbors the bottle-up emotions that lay dormant inside

And when this happens

The park is where I go to clear my mind

Walking the trail

Puts my mind at ease

And I love passing by the trees

Where the birds reside

Because their beautiful songs fill the sky

And the trees dwarf the pedestrians passing nearby

But of course, I also have to sit down and look up at the sky

Because I can stare at the clouds as they pass by

Taking the shape of the thoughts that run through my mind

I do this all the time

Because the park is where I go to clear my mind

When I die

I hope when I die

God forgives me for being speculative

I hope death is not an automatic

Predetermined destination

That before he casts judgment

He pulls me aside

And asks me if I accept him

Am I wrong for needing

To be offered a chance?

I hope when I die

Why I keep my distance

Some days I wish I could

Look at you

And not feel anything

A normal conversation

Among friends

But my heart wants

So much more than that

This is why I keep my distance

Limbo

I hope when I die

You'll be there

To greet me

In the afterlife

I'm fine with spending

A few decades in limbo

As long as you're

The first thing

I wake up to

We can never go back

What hurt me more than anything

Was looking into your eyes

And being instantly aware

Of the hurt I caused you

Knowing there's nothing I can do

To reverse it

And like a detective,

I'm forced to use de-escalation tactics

In hopes of salvaging what's left

But deep down, I know we can never go back

To the way things were

Before this moment

God

When I needed someone to
help heal my pain

No one came

I was all alone

Talking to the wall is what
granted me solace

Because when I closed my
eyes

In my mind, I could picture

Something inside

A being of this world

But not quite

Lurking somewhere parallel

An all-seeing eye

I could talk to and express

All I had buried inside

Acting as both my guide

And a friend

That never replied

But still somehow, I knew

What was meant of me

And I knew he had my back

For eternity

Generic love poem

If I had to

Write a generic poem about you,

It would begin with

Roses are red

Violets are blue

But I wouldn't even be able

To make it halfway through

Before dropping the pen

And realizing I could never go through with

Writing such a poem

Especially about you

Because what's the point when

I didn't even have to think it through?

Preventing me from feeling the same way I do

When next to you

Losing

It took losing everything

To give me the push needed

To make positive changes

To remain invisible

To be a creep

Is to not be seen as attractive as the next man

It's to have your heart in the right place

And put forth the maximum

Amount of effort

But be treated as having done nothing at all

It's to be the one that people talk about

So, the ones you act as the scapegoat for

Can remain invisible

In the midst of loneliness

In the midst of loneliness

She saw what she thought
was a glimpse of true
happiness

A way to finally relinquish
the constant sadness

And in this, she sought in the
embodiment of a man

Not knowing she had to come
to grips with herself to truly
begin

Never stopping for a moment
to think if she was just letting
the sense

Of false security

Reel her in

After all, he appeared as a
tall, gentle, handsome man

But bore a strange aura

That sometimes presented an
uneasy feeling towards her

But she could not bring
herself to label them as

Small warnings

Because sometimes the signs
are harder to recognize

When despair is what guides
your mind

And so, it was with this
decision

That for quite some time

Lust was granted a mistaken
identity

And allowed to remain in
plain sight

Giving her the pretense that
this is what love was like

An imitation of the prize

I wish I got the chance to see

What me and you could have been

But you were only there to serve as a tutorial

To walk me through the different stages

You gave me those initial feelings

And showed me what it was to love another person

To trust

And open my heart up to them

But at the same time, I failed to see

That this was all training

You were the imitation of the prize at the end

A premonition of what there could be

The whole time you were building me up,

So, I could find this with someone else

I learned that after you showed me

How heartbreak felt

Toxic love

I was born to a pair

Addicted to the chaos of one another

Trying desperately to fulfill a fantasy of being more than lovers

They really did think they truly loved each other

The constant fighting and cheating however was no bother

Because in the end, they would always find themselves back
together

Too blinded by the lust and excitement

To just take a second and ask why?

And in a desperate attempt to convert their feelings of lust

Into those of love

Decided to conceive

Giving life to a corrupted seed

That would from then on

Serve as the only thing linking them to each other

I have finally found what I seek

There's a flash of light

And a loud scream heard in the middle of the night

A bullet pierces my heart

And I am greeted by a bright light

I fade away like the whisper of a breeze

I become the trees and the fruit that grows from the seeds

I'm the color that covers the leaves

And I'm the soil that's underneath

After so many years of searching for peace

In death, I have finally found what I seek

A mark

It hurts for me to look at you

Knowing that in the end

The history we shared together

Held little value to you

The memories I reminisce about every day

Don't cross your mind

Whether it be the smiles or laughs we exchanged

Or just simply being in each other's presence

Our existence was simply a mark on your memory

Something that could be erased

A barrier of understanding

Have you ever been around that person

That makes life appear more in depth than it was?

For instance

An activity you would otherwise find very rudimentary

Is all of a sudden granted a new meaning

Like all of its intricate inner workings

Have just been revealed to you

And you are imbued with the culture

And everything that surrounds it

You are finally able to see what everyone else has been seeing

And you start to wonder about

What else you might not understand the full gravity of

Fantasies

Fantasies

At times

I thought I could see glimpses

Of a common interest

But I've always had a habit

Of reading too much into things

I'm easily invested in fantasies

Ugly

Ugly has been a good friend to me

I have been blessed with beauty

Only the truest can see

And so,

I am never deceived

And even if I must sail the sea of misery,

I know it is true beauty

That beats for me

After loving you

I can never be the same

You left me broken

With remnants of my previous existence

Scattered

Beyond the depths of my reach

Far enough to leave me

With little resemblance

Of my past self

But close enough

To give me something to long for

How thoughtful

I'm sorry

It was wrong for me to expect

So much of you

I wanted you to fight for me

Knowing you had never

Fought for anyone before

All I needed

I fell in love with the thought of

What it would be like

To be with you

And it was all I needed

A fantasy I could live comfortably in

Without the possible ramifications of

What would have happened

Had I told you

How I felt

How it is to love the unlovable

I share with you my heart

So that you may tear it apart

I reveal my most vulnerable self

So that you may exploit it

I show an outgoing helping hand

So that you may abuse it

And amidst the confusion

I lose myself

Another lesson

In my mind,

A statue of you was erected

Upon an already occupied foundation

Despite weeks of planning and preparation

In an effort to become self-reliant

I guess I'm not quite ready for that part yet

I just hope you're not another lesson on why

I should have waited

The letters I write

The letters I write

Always seem to find a way to swallow themselves

In amongst my frustrated palms might

Tossed and scattered around like decorations

Illuminated by the soft candlelight

My frustration mounting as new words come to mind

Being plotted and rearranged on every line

But still

It is the right ones I can never find

The quick dance of the pen

Helping to commemorate in short spurts

What I wish to iterate

Before those too

Become subjected to the same fate

And then out goes the flame

Separate entities

It's still so weird to me

How now we are separate entities

We no longer exist

In the world we created together

The moments we shared

Replaced with dormant representations

Of what had once been

Phantom pains, as if I've lost a limb

Memories brought on by the incense of your perfume

Engraved into my mind

It's funny how this world revolved around you

At one point in time

Imagine

Sometimes I imagine what it would be like

For our relationship to end

I hope I'm not just another memory

You can push towards the dark recesses of your mind

And never have to worry about it resurfacing again

I want our chapter to have meant more than that

Even if it means you have to hate me

For it to happen

At least then I'd know I had an effect

And maybe even helped steer you in the right direction

Hopefully towards someone truly worthy

Who can offer you more than I ever could

That's how much I love you

A place within

When we are broken down

And feeling worn

We make ourselves a little
place in our hearts

Where we can feel warm

A little place where we feel
safe

And with every ounce of
strength

We call on from within

And pray that the door will
open once again

Because each time it gets
harder to get in

For me

This door leads to a little
house surrounded by
shrubbery

To escape to

A little place where I can step
onto the porch

And feed the birds

Or step outside

To tend to the trees

But for you, that may be a
little different

For we are all unique

But I always thank God for
letting me back in

Because I would have surely
lost it

If I didn't have this place
within

I hope my moments of weakness

Don't make me anything less than human

I can't help how I feel about you

But you're not supposed to be in love with your friends

I wish I would have kept it hidden

But I will continue to take it one day at a time

Until I get back to being

The friend I'm supposed to be

Finally free

I could hear the birds and their sweet songs

The smell of spring

Oh, how I longed

Longed for the smell of the trees and the soft breeze

I was kept away for so long

My house nearly gone

Covered in snow

Winter had been consumed by the cold

The thought of finally being free brought me to my knees

I was finally free after being stuck in that house for so long

And so, I just sat there and listened to the birds sweet songs

But as I looked up at the sky

Something caught my eye

A snowflake had landed nearby

Time 2

A while has passed

Since I last experienced

The magic of an entire day

Being felt in mere moments

Because when with you

Time would feel accelerated

And I would often find
myself

When the end of the day
approached

Looking towards the moon

Wondering when we should
stop talking

Because a new day was
coming

Back then

Relishing in time used to feel
meaningless

Because it was something
that felt almost endless

And it never once crossed my
mind

As something that should be
cherished

But now that time has begun
to slow

I take the time needed to
relish in every minute

While every now and then

Allowing myself a few
moments

To glance into the past

And relive lost hours passed

And I know that now

While I can no longer
experience your smile

I can still put to use

The lessons I learned from
you

About time

And maybe then

Down the road

Time can bestow with me

A new smile

Depression

Is when yesterday

Is the only day of the week

Extension

You are just as much of an extension of me

As I am you

Why do we act like we're so different?

236

Desensitized

I'm desensitized to my emotions

I approach everything

With the same calmness

There's a barrier between us

And I wonder if you'll ever be able

To see past it

I couldn't show you the way

Even if I tried

I'm trapped inside my mind

I hope you care enough to

Maneuver through this hurdle blind

And show me the way

To the other side

The day she left

Is when it all changed

The sky became my eyes

And every time it rained

I would cry

The rain came down with a passion

Thick and heavy

And the droplets bitter

Because when she left

She took part of me with her

I want to be the first to go

When it's time for me to die

I want to be the first to go

Because in terms of being

Left alone

I don't even want to know

Options

There are no second places in love

Nothing has changed

Since our last interaction

I'm still the same person

But why is it that now

You are suddenly interested?

When you had options

I didn't exist

Exiled

Why is it I struggle with being lonesome

Despite my heart always being open?

Free to approach by anyone that may be wandering

Because I know how hard it is

When you have no one

But perhaps these feelings come from being exiled

And not knowing

Searching until you find that person

With their heart too

Open

Leaf in the wind

Every day goes by

Without a sense of arrival

I'm a leaf in the wind

With no sense of direction

Exaggerated feelings

No one notices the days I don't eat

Or the nights I don't sleep

But everyone seems to already know

How to handle each situation accordingly

They talk as if there is a magic off switch

I'm just not seeing

And by yelling

They are helping point me in the right direction

If only it were as simple as flipping a switch

To get rid of "exaggerated feelings"

Forwards

Sometimes I wish I had no recollection of the day before

So that every day I would be looking forward

Because I spend too much time looking back

Dwelling on the past

Wishing I could alter what can't be changed

And sometimes I wish that people would forget my name

Because I would rather be a nameless face

Than people only remembering my name

Because of the embarrassing mistakes I've made

Life is a fickle thing

life is a fickle, merry thing

That oozes with personality

As creator

I could not deter

From any one thing

And be asked upon which

Objectively define it

In its entirety

It is too robust for

Any one definition

The drive from dreams

Sometimes I like to wish for things

I don't want to achieve

Because it's that feeling of wanting

That allows me to dream

And push through

In times of need

And to achieve would mean to

Forgo the drive it brings me

So, when I find myself in situations

Where the outcome feels out of reach

I always dream

What of time?

What of time?

Every second gone by

Is a miniscule drop in a bucket

As long as we do not allow it

To reach the point of overflowing

There is no such thing

As a wasted moment

Bask in every second

We never know whether or not

It'll be the last time

We are able to experience

Moments like this

No longer the victim

I had the key, but I still couldn't free myself

I had the means to end this

But I hesitated

I could not go through with it

I was trapped

The lock kept shifting

Changing

The room morphing to his every command

Making the walls close in

He left the key only to toy with me

To provoke me

But I could not let him get to me

I had to fight it

Let him know that he could not control me

And so, with every ounce of strength

I finally stopped being his victim and became his enemy

Fountain of youth

Everyone around me

Seems to have become

Accustomed to their age

But I'm still stuck in limbo

Trying to figure out

How to navigate towards

That stage

Perhaps I have stumbled upon

The fountain of youth

Dust in the wind

I wish I could reach into my being

And show you that I am aware

Of the situation

That has warranted

The response I am receiving

I can see the subtle changes

In our interactions

But how can I address this

When I'm the main cause of it?

I've crossed a line I shouldn't have

Needed to be told about

I've reached the point of no return

And now I am dust in the wind

Cast aside by the breeze

I was the sky

As soon as you left

Rain began to pour

And as thoughts of you continued to cross my mind

The clouds had decided to aid me

During this time

The rain was granted consent

And allowed to disperse through my pores

Expelling warm tears

Every time thoughts of you drew near

But deep inside a storm had begun to slowly form

And over the course of a few days

This only seemed to heighten

So, the clouds allowed me to borrow the thunder and lightning

In exchange for their guidance

This entire time

I was the sky

Self-aware

Maybe I'm too self-aware

To reap the benefits

Of ignorance

I scour every argument

In search of known routes

But often end up

Exploring backroads and unmarked trails

Never willing to take a firm stance

On any one direction

I wonder if I'll ever

Find where it is I'm going

Do I regret it?

Sometimes I wonder if it was a mistake to let my feelings be known

The anxiety of telling you had my mind racing

But the smile given to me by the thought of the possibility

Still gave me hope

So, I thought *let them be known*

But now I seem to have lost my ability to speak to you

Without using notes

And this is quite the setback

Seeing how we were so close

And never before did I have to worry about holding my tongue

But now it seems there's a hint of uneasiness in your words

Especially seeing as now I'm the only one that messages first

But do I regret it?

No

The long descent

Time and time again,

I thought that I have come close to

Reaching the end

But as I look down, I realize

I haven't even begun to move

From where I had began

As I travel down the slope

I hear her voice again

And I end up at the peak again

On top of the footsteps

Left previously

By my own man

Seemingly never moving

From where I had began

The sound of her voice putting my mind

At a perpetual state of decline

<h1 style="text-align:center">A dreadful day</h1>

You came to me

In the midst of

A dreadful day

And now I must

Sit back and observe

The way my speech

Forever frozen in time,

Dictates

The momentum of our relationship

Going forward

Opposite

When we die,

I hope we become the opposite

Of what we were during life

So, I can see what it's like

On the other side

Maybe then I will understand why

Me and you

Were never meant to be

Best-case scenario

I discover we are eternal opposites

worst-case scenario

I still fall for you

The greatest peace

I wonder if my dreams

Is really the only place where me and you

Can exist simultaneously

And if so,

Why am I given this glimpse?

As if the thought of it

Can somehow be made a possibility

Maybe that's just me hoping to make it so

In this reality

But what if what I really see

Is me

Hoping to make it seen

That in another reality

I have already conquered this feat

And now I have the closure needed

To pursue things differently

Finally, I have peace

Wasteland

My mind was too barren

Of a wasteland

To recognize the significance

Of being bearer of your insignia

A mind ripe for the conversion of a kingdom

Forged copies of paintings

Unknowingly lined the walls

Of the rooms you occupied

My heart belongs to an

Unknown artist

Goodbye

I hope before you say goodbye

Our souls hug

One last time

Never give up

You only have one life to live

So, you might as well

See this thing out

If thing go bad,

Then things go bad

It's all part of the experience

Closing

Closing

Thank you to everyone for joining me on this journey. This is something I have been dedicated to for a long time and I'm glad to have made it this far. This journey has had a lot of ups and downs and I hope my work has showcased that. I hope you all have enjoyed my work so far and I hope I have a real future at this. I love you all.

-Alex

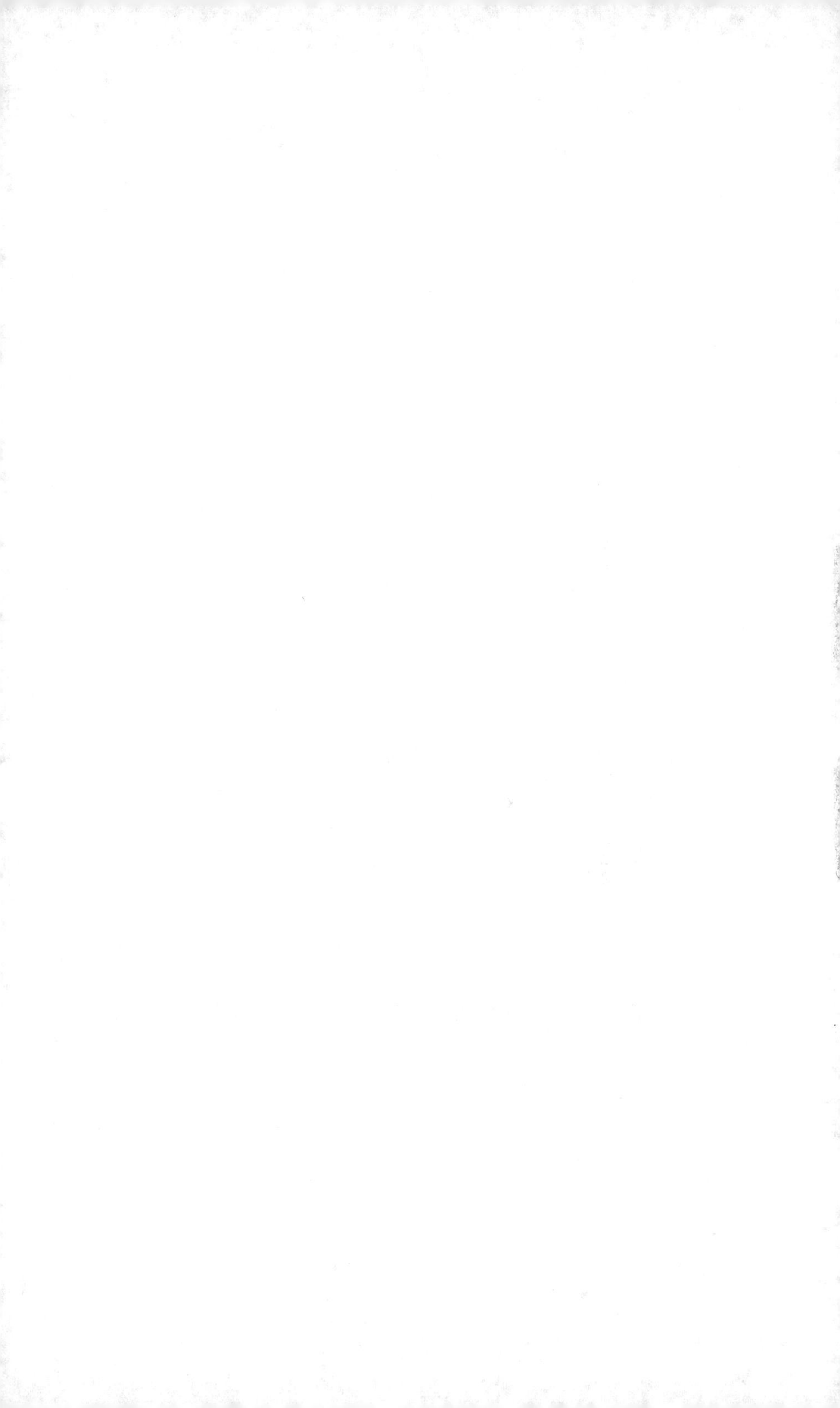

www.ingramcontent.com/pod-product-compliance
Lightning Source LLC
Chambersburg PA
CBHW072210150726
48002CB00005B/1746